MW01245600

A Voice, A Soul, A Man Speaks

Words spoken through the eyes of a
Black Man living in Baltimore City navigating
his faith, new love and challenges and
struggles as a single father of three.
My past did not speak for my future,
I don't need a "Million Men" to know that!

TYRA J. ROBINSON, SR.

Published in the United States of America

Brilliant Books Literary
137 Forest Park Lane Thomasville
North Carolina 27360 USA

ISBN:
Paperback: 979-8-88945-207-2
E-book: 979-8-88945-208-9
Hardback: 979-8-88945-209-6

"A False Call of Concern"

Have you ever been put on the shelf for
someone always trying but never doing?

They look in your eyes see your displeasure yet
they give you nothing better to smile about.

You walk out the room face full of gloom...

Then you get it!

You get the call of concern, you let up, let out then—it's on.

What seemed to be caring and not that it wasn't is the
FALSE CALL OF CONCERN to open you up
and beat you down.

You trust, believe, and honor just to feel you have
turned the gun on yourself and pulled the trigger!

It's O.K., relationships are like that.

But to be a man and to trust a woman,
to receive that call takes nerves
but so beware one time too many can be
a FALSE CALL OF CONCERN!

Only to get into your head and leave you feeling
guilty and that's a concern always.

THE STRUGGLE II

The struggle is it forever
Will one ever overcome it
To you it's never
To go all day and at any time fail
The shame and ugliness you feel in the inside
Trivial as opportunities may seem stale
You go through a season of peace
You forget who delivered you
All that was deceased has increased and risen
The victory seems not won
The wrong desires start to burn
Get back to the plan, be more dedicated
And this time punctuate it with faith, hope and believing
The Struggle is over do not climb to victory, climb from victory,
struggle is your ladder

CONNECTION

Sockets and cords make a quick current a spark
Lips to lips make love a great fit…KISS
Need no perfection for a good connection
The head bone connected to the neckbone
Broken hearts and lights not working
Sparkplugs and flowers will do to get the moment going and ignited
An old connection reunited
At a prayers request on separation from your maker
You need this connection to be whole within
To commune and belong in the noon of the day as the sun shines
On its flowers and rain pours its storm
Neglection of snow doesn't matter, bird's chit chatter,
little children's laughter
Can it get better or even greater a selection of days and events
Giving one the connection of life!

TYRA J. ROBINSON, SR.

STOP WEEPING

Stop weeping He's not dead
Stop feeling sad, get out bed
Jesus is alive shout Hallelujah
Give praise to God for all He's done for you!

You cry because you can't have your way
You burst into tears over past hurt years
Carrying the burdens of life's distress
Can't get over countless failed test

Stop your weeping He has risen
God has forgiven so listen, let your heart glisten
Wipe your eyes don't cry
Dry your tears Jesus is here!

Stop your weeping
He's not sleeping any more
You can rejoice we got the Victory
Jesus has made history

So   Weep   No   More   Because   Jesus   Has   Risen!

THE COST OF DISCIPLESHIP

Jesus said pick up your cross and follow me
You must not love some others to be my disciple
In this place of life you must deny your own life
Bare your cross and never put it down
So that the lost may be found

Am I teacher or master?
Who do you follow and come after?
Do take a rest
It's the most crucial time in a test Instead of giving your best

Not your father, mother, sister, or even brother
Should hinder your baring
Your heart for the kingdom must be despairing

What do you count as a lost in this walk with me?
What do you give up?
What do you let go of?
What, what do you put on the soul of the unsaved or
Next of kin

Just follow Jesus and he will make you fishers of men
But don't look back to go eat, drink and bury the dead
The cost of discipleship rest ahead
So BARE YOUR CROSS INSTEAD

EMPTINESS WITHOUT GOD

A hard heart
Feeling cold in the inside
Good times make you want to run inside
You're empty inside

You turn to, to friends who don't need you
You confide in drinking and all to fulfill your emptiness
Never satisfied so you lie
Money always running out, the more you make the less you have
You say you believe in God but there's no evidence of Him in
your life

You always have the largest crowd and the biggest car but inside
you're all alone
You eat but are never full and success is never enough
You have plenty of covers but never are warm
You long for fulfilment and who you can trust
You are so tired you need God—a Savior

God can fill the void and exchange your heart of stone for a
heart of flesh
You'll never be alone again because God is your Strong Tower
He is always home… you will not suffer again
No more emptiness without God

God Knows Best

Have you ever waited for an answer from God?
Did He give you signs and dreams and wonders?
What did He mean when He sent them?
Deep inside is it what you wanted?

But did it ever cross your mind, it didn't
You pray, pray, pray and believe in your faith
Just to find out it's not going your way
Well I did!

I need the ministry and I need it a lot
Yet what I asked for takes away from that a lot
At times I saw my double tongue compromising
on what I believe and stood for all along

Yes I was disappointed when He didn't come through
But I should have known
I always pray for His way and will

I'm over it now but still a little embarrassed
or ashamed because I believed it had my name all over it

I do believe the thing I asked God for was not best for me even
though I wanted it to be. His best will keep me in line, test
my faith and build my character and times
as it is, it is working in me now.

My Father God knows best for me even when
my will and desire set my prayers a fire
God knows best and that He cares for my life!!!

SERVICE

The arm service
The car need service
Life a disservice
Is this making you nervous

To serve the people
To give all you have of yourself
Pouring into another vessel Service is good for your health

The family service
The husband and wife service
Community service
Or maybe customer service

Where do you serve?
When will you serve?
How can you serve?
Who will you serve?

Whatever you decide, you are going to serve someone or
something!

Resting In Peace

Resting In Peace
Peace that last forever,
A sleep that's calm as the wind
Who do you look for and where did they go?
I'm suggesting their resting in peace

Oh death, where is thy sting
Thy ring is upon your head
Live with Christ instead
Because the just are not dead

No more pain for gain
Nor crying and being mistreated
Even family members using me and being conceited
I'm asleep now or one day I'll be resting in peace

Many have gone before me out of the world, they go
Into thy presence of the Lord for sure
Now they can smile all the time, joy never ending
What a wonderful friend in Jesus they have!
No more testing or grief for the rest of eternity it's resting in peace

TYRA J. ROBINSON, SR.

WALKING ON THE WATER

Jesus walked on the water
Peter did too
You can walk on the water if you believe too

Walking on the water is a tall feat
Ever in a storm, walking on the water is not the norm
So take one step onto the water

You can walk on the water
I can walk on the water
Fix your eyes on Jesus and walk!
ON THE WATER!

So get your faith moving
Take the step of faith
Get yourself in order
Focus on Jesus
And then you'll be walking on the water

INWARD RENEWAL

Outside I look great
Inside there's bruises everywhere
Outside you see a bright smile
Inside a sad face of shame

A makeover for sure must take place
They say I have a good heart
I tell you the truth my heart aches for GOD
HE's been giving me a heart transplant

The surgery is forever
Yet if you look at me, you'll say he's fine
I do want the change, but it hurts in the inside
On the outside, I have joy

But on the inside humility is shaping
My heart is larger
I can forgive because I've been forgiven
Each day gets brighter than before

I have a jewel in me now, I must keep it safe
There's a robber always trying to break in
He wants me to fall, fail, flip over, and faint
He can't have me back, I've moved on

I've been changed for the better
And I won't look back, I won't give up
Because I'm on higher ground
I've been pulled from the pool of inward renewal

I NEED GOD

I need GOD when things are going good
Where are you GOD?
Are YOU in my presence or are YOU going to and fro?

I need you GOD!
Can I see YOUR face?
I can see YOUR work cause I'm a piece of work
Are YOU listening to my prayers

I need GOD
I need YOU GOD in my situations positive and negative
Can I find YOU to share my pain?
Did I miss YOU calling my name?

I'm calling YOU in the day, afternoon, evening
and in the midnight hour
I need YOU and I'm very excited
Can I meet YOU at the table of host?
GOD help YOUR child, I need YOU!

A Voice, A Soul, A Man Speaks

I need YOU for comfort
I need YOU for companionship
I need YOU for faith
I need YOU for love
I need YOU for Salvation
I need YOU for Miracles
I need YOU to be GOD!!!

TIMING

Waiting on time cause timing is everything
From the time I wake up in the morning
To the time I go to bed
Timing is everything

Got to hurry and get to work
I can't be late because timing is everything
Timing have you noticed it's so important
Time to eat dinner and time to eat lunch if I choose

But there's always time for breakfast
Time to make time for GOD
Time to party as if all day wouldn't be ok
Time to fix dinner

All time is given to the kids
To kid's time is forever and ever
Why worry its only time
Yes, it's only time that's a problem

A Voice, A Soul, A Man Speaks

Time doesn't worry it will leave and ask later
    What happened and where were you and so on
        And you'll say or on the other hand blame time
            You can't blame time because in time, time will tell

You may tell on time first, yet time always has the final say
    Time is in GOD's hand's we get 24 a day
        So, your life means everything because GOD holds it
            Cause timing especially GOD's timing is everything

TYRA J. ROBINSON, SR.

GOD'S GRACE

A Christian searching for love
I've done everything wrong on this side of Heaven
Even I at times hate my place
Yet it is only because of God's Grace

He's given me all that I need
Whether I deserve it or not His Grace is a blessing
I thank Him much for all He's done
I even ask for restoration, it's in His reputation

Even in the darkest place God's Grace will find you
If I lose pace
Or catching an unfortunate case
My God continues to pour out His Grace

It feels my being with mercy and love
All from His hand that comes from above
One day I'll see His face
God is Grace

MY FATHER ANSWERS!

He's quick fast and never late
Yet sometimes he'll have you to wait
I myself ask Him for everything
From water to riches and yes pulling me out of ditches

Oh yes true, sometimes He lets me go through
I always come out stronger and better prepared
Lately I'm asked for my heart's desire small or large
He hasn't denied me, has met the need

The old folks say He may not come when you want Him
But He's always right on time
Yes, that is true in itself, I don't use that one
Since I try Him often for myself

Everything I asked in prayer I speak it as though it true
Quickly every prayer has been answered to date, I tell for sure
He is never late
Often early if its according to His will, that must be it
A plan, a purpose to ask the FATHER thy will be done

Yes, it's true some hasn't happened yet
Or is it He's waiting to surprise me with more of Him I'll get
I've prayed for the spiritual, physical, emotional, and financial
and anything else you can think of I'll have

Listen all who must know my Father in Heaven
longs to give me more
I know I haven't seen nothing yet, as long as I fix my eyes on
JESUS count on the breakthrough
I know I don't deserve it but for all my FATHER does is
ANSWERS when I call

THE VISION

The vision of your youth
Now your older you have no proof
A seed sown day's afar
Dream crashers who they are

Even at 10 the vision fights for life
What part do you play determines the outcome
Even in your teens you can see its growth
You can see the weeds of life choking it from behind

At adult stage life jumps on with rage
But it's o.k. your grown up now
No one can let you down
And the vision is still alive

Now you're in your 30's
What are you seeing now
The start comes pass
Yet the fight comes on fast
Because life's decisions destroys and decays visions

It is real
It is true
It is pure and plain
Receiving the vision is a whole life's gain

I FEEL IT!

I FEEL IT MY BONES!
I FEEL IT IN MY FEET!
I FEEL IT IN MY HEART!
I JUST CAN'T SLEEP

I KNOW ITS COMING
VERY SOON THAT IS
A PHONE CALL AND ALL THAT
I FEEL IT COMING

HERE IT IS
THERE IT GOES
BREATHE!
IT'S MY BREATH
OKAY STAY CALM
I FEEL IT......

I CAN'T FILL IT
ITS NOT A FEELING
ITS FRUIT
ITS CALLED PEACE!

DEACON

You stand tall at the door to lead
The wisdom you give heed righteousness
Who wouldn't want to listen
You're well respected and known

Deacon your so polite and CHRIST like
I want to know did you walk on water last night
Always making time in your busy schedule
That's because you care

Such a great listener
For one can talk forever, HA HA HA
The people you help you encourage to great lengths
You are a Deacon

So, keep on speaking
Helping the saints along the rugged road
Because you are needed in the kingdom
You are Deacon

TYRA J. ROBINSON, SR.

ENOUGH IS ENOUGH

Enough of these halfhearted prayers
These double-double dares
Telling GOD my needs once a week
That's if I even speak

The praises go up the blessings come down
Yet I haven't seen GOD around
My knees are beautiful
Shook I haven't bent down yet

Going through the same old same old
Today righteous GOD will know
Consistent and diligent I will be
I will pray till HE answers me

I'm sick and tired of being sick and tired
Yet I'm blessed, but in my spirit, I know it is not GOD's best
I came to and through I'm going after my breakthrough
I used to huff and puff, think I was tough
JESUS was enough

But today and yesterday the sermon said I needed to shush
And lift the LORD up
Cause enough is enough

Enough is enough as enough can be I fall to thy knees to talk to
JESUS bless me please!

A HEARTS DESIRE

What I desire I asked for
What I needed I got first
Yet I thank HIM
But still I thirst

> The first is a testing
> The second is a blessing
> Yet small but satisfying
> Even bigger yet desiring

> > Oh truly it was my hearts desire
> > As HE shows and tells me, my inner is on fire
> > I can't believe, yet still I do hope the hand of
> > GOD moves
> > I humble myself, felt with joy

> > > I take it in and say to myself
> > > That means another storm
> > > Oh yes and another blessing
> > > So I pray again and to my GOD and
> > > tell HIM all things

> > > > While that is going on the
> > > > spirit is searching all things
> > > > So I can expect GOD to do a
> > > > new thing Hallelujah!

Tyra J. Robinson, Sr.

HAVE MERCY ON
A SINNER

The repentant prayer,
The most powerful of words to carry before GOD
Lord have mercy on me a sinner
This phrase is a life changing phrase
Have mercy on me a sinner for the thoughts of deceit
Have mercy on me a sinner for not giving YOU the praise and
myself the glory
Have mercy on me a sinner for passing the poor by
Have mercy on me a sinner for disobeying YOUR word
Have mercy on me a sinner for withholding love
Have mercy on me a sinner for not living right
Have mercy on me a sinner for not sharing your light
Have mercy on me a sinner for not fellowshipping with CHRIST

A Voice, A Soul, A Man Speaks

Have mercy on me a sinner for always believing I'm right
Have mercy on me a sinner for doing half the job
Have mercy on me a sinner for touching which is holy
Have mercy on me a sinner for lack of compassion
Have mercy on me a sinner for not putting my faith into action
Have mercy on me a sinner because I
need you to make me complete
Have mercy on me a sinner because I'm tired of defeat
Have mercy on me a sinner because I don't deserve your grace
Have mercy on me a sinner because I wish to change my place
Have mercy on me a sinner because I'm tired and will not rest
Have mercy on me a sinner, I surrender LORD
to YOU because YOU know best
Give mercy and grace to this sinner so that thee may rest
Amen.

TYRA J. ROBINSON, SR.

THE HAND OF GOD

The hand of GOD is too big for me to shake
He touches the whole world and it awakes
For when I fall lest I fall I slip I've never hit the ground
Because the hand of GOD was there

When I was sick the hand of GOD took care of me
He gave me love and the medicine I needed to be healed
I know it was the hand of GOD
Sometimes I make a wrong turn
Yet all the dead ends turn me back right to the starting point

That's the road I was traveling
The thing is, is that I lost time, I wasn't ahead, but on schedule
I believe it was the hand of GOD
When I'm so excited because of a sudden change

I glorify the name of the LORD because of the move of
HIS mighty hand
I understand now that I can't hide from HIS hand it moves
everything out of sight
I can take steps of faith; because the hand of GOD its always moving
The tender hand of GOD cares and disciplines me for HE's my
FATHER

A Voice, A Soul, A Man Speaks

HE takes my heart and protects it and ensures me no heartache
And yet the one thing that is certain the hand of GOD mean's
HE's always shaping me
Changing me, molding me because he is the expert crafts men
How awesome is the hand of GOD

Mighty, Strong, Powerful, Soft, Swift and outstretched to those
whom HE loves
That's the hand of GOD

A FRIEND

It is true a friend is someone who sticks closer than a brother
A friend loves through all times, miles, storms and pains
A friend can break your heart
A friend can give you a new heart
What a friend I have

Without a friend your alone in this world
A friend can be anybody
A friend can be your mom, dad, brother, sister, neighbor, anybody
Friends will turn their backs on you, betray you,
slay you and hate you
Whether it's your fault or theirs somebody got to be
the friend who cares
They say friendship are a dime a dozen but someone who sticks
closer than a brother is one in a million
Sometimes there's no one to turn to but a friend in mind

A friend can leave a wrinkle in time
A friend will put up with your mess, they'll listen to the same
stories you tell over and over again and treat it likes it the first time
I have found a friend like that of mine on this earth
No matter what I'll love my friends and my friend to
beginning and end
That's having a friend

There's no other than a friend that's sticks closer than a brother

I LOVE YOU

I LOVE YOU
WHO ARE YOU THAT I LOVE
WHAT IS THE LOVE THAT I HAVE FOR YOU
I LOVE YOU

NOT FOR YOUR MONEY
MAYBE BECAUSE YOU'RE FUNNY
DON'T THINK IT'S BECAUSE OF YOUR OUTWARD
APPEARANCE
I'M LOOKING FOR YOUR INNER EXPERIENCE
I LOVE YOU

I LOVED YOU SINCE DAY ONE
NOT FOR YOUR KNOWLEDGE OR POTENTIAL
BUT FOR THE ENTANGABLES YOU BRING
I LOVE YOU JUST NOT FOR TODAY
I HAVEN'T EVEN CONSIDERED LOVE FOR TOMORROW

BECAUSE I WISH NOT TO BORROW
ON AN UP IN SORROW, BECAUSE TOMORROW IS NOT
PROMISE
YET TODAY IS WHAT I'VE BEEN GIVEN
SO I'M DRIVEN FOR TODAY
YESTERDAY IS A TREASURE IN MY CHEST

THAT'S YESTERDAY LOVE, MAKES TODAY EVEN SWEETER
I LOVE YOU
WHO ARE YOU THAT I LOVE
WHAT IS THE LOVE I HAVE FOR YOU
YOU LOVE ME
I LOVE YOU

WE LOVE EACH OTHER
I LOVE YOUR HEART
I LOVE YOUR SOUL

I LOVE YOUR MIND
I LOVE YOUR SPRIT
I LOVE YOUR BODY
I LOVE YOUR SELFWORTH

I LOVE YOU

WHAT I'M WAITING FOR

I'm sitting here writing my prayer list
It is full of wants, needs and desires
I fill the pages left to right
How long must I wait, I will tire

Some prayers have been answered over and over
Some prayers have yet to come to pass
But the majority are in the making
Blessing I long for are here for the taking

All kinds of prayers I pray
I pray for family, friends, wife, healing, lots more
I pray that doors will open and doors will close
Yet I pray in believing that GOD knows me best
The bible says the spirit of a man murmurs before GOD,
because we know not what we ask when we pray

I tell you no lie I'm waiting on the LORD
I'm waiting on me
I'm even waiting on my deliverance
I ask, LORD come by here, oh LORD come by here

TYRA J. ROBINSON, SR.

But you are what I hear a whole lot of
What am I waiting for
I'm waiting on GOD I tell them
I tell myself I'm waiting on GOD

The enemy always ask me what am I waiting on
I tell him in JESUS I already have it
Only one thing to wait on is my LORD's return
That's what and who I'm waiting for

SPEAK TO ME, BROTHER!

Brother where art thou
I need your ever presence
Brother you were around when things got tough
I call you endlessly, endlessly I call you

Brother where you been
you know your not just my brother but also a friend
Brother this is hard times
This world would not let me get ahead

Oh brother speak a word to change my mood
Brother you're important to me
You are the standard of encouragement
Every word you speak opens doors from imprisonment

Every word is well seasoned like southern fried fish
I can tell before you speak you cleanse and season it all I can't
wait to get served
Brother you're not just a member of the family
You're there through trials, test, death, and the victory

Thank you brother for when you speak
Oh my brother speak to me a word
That will ease the pain and the hurt
That will have no more dominion over me

Our brother, your brother, let the way that your word's multiply
speak time into us my brother!

TYRA J. ROBINSON, SR.

CREAM

I scream you scream
We all scream out of our dreams for cream
What a word and its bold meaning
Only to believe it and its meaning

As the preacher once taught
And declared a mighty, mighty word
That nothing is greater than cream
Oh that Sunday Holy service
Cream the preacher screamed
Only to wonder what he meant

Doesn't it sound good to my ears
Doesn't it taste good to my spirit
Doesn't it make me rejoice when I hear it
Doesn't it make me cry as it pierces my heart

The worship is almost over, the preacher is on his point number 5
The congregation ecstatic with praise
The sound of worship filling the place
The spirit moving on hearts as the word ministers to the church

I scream, you scream CHRIST Rules Everything Around Me
Cream, yes that's what it means we scream!

YOU'LL FIND HIM

Who do you seek
What do you want
Have you found what you're looking for
I've heard you're very rich

The people who know you lift you up
Even at home you are empty
You buy cars, clothes anything you want
You could lie and no one could care
Because to them you have
They want it

You go to church
You tithe
You love your neighbor
But yet you yourself haven't found it

What do you seek
What do you want
Have you asked
But you have everything

Listen to the knock
Answer the door
Because the answer is here
No more emptiness, false joy, I got it all show
Now going to church is not just a childhood practice

Now your richer than ever
Now the look is in you
Now all you wanted,you give
Now you have rest tonight because you have found HIM

DON'T NEGLECT WAITING

Have you ever waited for an important phone call
Only to never receive it
Can you just imagine a beautiful sunrise
Only to watch as the clouds cover it

You knocked and knocked and no one answered
Yet you hear the watching of tv behind the close doors
Or maybe its time just ticking away
Still your day hasn't come

I'm sure you prayed diligently
I'm sure you focused earnestly
I'm sure you hope never failed
Still you thought GOD failed you

You thought mother, father, sister, brother just about everybody
had let you down
You waited pass your wits end
You slept on it to get away from what you were seeing
Holding on to a glimmer of faith

Then all of sudden the clouds moved
and sun came reaching out
Then all of sudden the phone rang and it was her
Then all of sudden you had so many blessings pouring from
heaven you
had no room to receive them all
Then all of sudden every prayer was getting answered

In time doors were opening
You started walking and no more running
You remember next time to prepare your-
self and make a decision
That you will not NEGLECT WAITING

A VOICE, A SOUL, A MAN SPEAKS

I'M A LEADER!

I'm a leader
So you say you're a leader?
So that means you are this.

A leader, leads by example.
A leader knows how to follow.
A true leader is a servant at heart.
So if you call yourself leader let's start.

Have you washed your follower's feet?
Have you turned the other cheek?
Did you sit at the Master's feet?

Have you sacrificed for good and all?
Have you given time, talent and treasure without thought?
Are you ashamed of who you are?

So leader are you a teacher by action and word?
So leader are you concerned about listening or being heard?
You love the label;
Are you peaceful in trouble times?
Is your light ever out when dark times returns?

So leader are you burning for love as much as to give love?
Or do you say I'm a leader just to be in charge.
You love the table, sit at the head of the table, receive the high praise.
When criticism comes you do not stand and take the blame.
You speaking I'm not doing that.

You still say I'm a leader Are you a LEADER?

TYRA J. ROBINSON, SR.

THE HEART OF MY REFLECTION

I saw my own reflection in a mirror;
I thought I was one of a kind
Now I see I am beautiful

A saw a very strange look upon my face
To touch my face is one thing
But to see me for myself had me wondering

I ask the reflection in the mirror
Who are you?
What do you want with me?
Most of all what are you steering at?

You know what that face said?
Shut up and listen
You over there have neglected me
You have not seen my hurt nor my shame
Yet you smile as though you see nothing wrong

A Voice, A Soul, A Man Speaks

Mirror I said, what is your problem?
If it weren't for me you could not tell a thing
The mirror said it's not a reflection of your face
The mirror said it's the reflection of your heart

I said to the reflection in the mirror
I'm sorry I cried to the reflection in the mirror
I touched the reflection in the mirror

The mirror said stop, if you don't know me from the inside
You'll never see yourself from the outside
So reflection next time I'll be ready because I know who you are
Reflection no more neglection

YOU CALL YOURSELF A CHRISTIAN

You call yourself a Christian because
you go to church on Sunday
You call yourself a Christian because
you know a bible verse or two
You call yourself a Christian because your bible totin'
You call yourself a Christian because
you show up Easter Sunday
You call yourself a Christian because you
bless your food when at home
You call yourself a Christian because you say a prayer at night
You call yourself a Christian because you
know there's a God and that's alright
You call yourself a Christian because you hum a hymn or two
You call yourself a Christian because you call on
God above when you're going through
Do you call yourself a Christian when Sunday has passed by
Do you call yourself a Christian when
hanging with your friends

A Voice, A Soul, A Man Speaks

Do you call yourself a Christian when
it's time for tithes and offerings
Do you call yourself a Christian when
God's calling you to change
Do you call yourself a Christian when everything is ok
Do you call yourself a Christian when you eat in a public place
Do you call yourself a Christian when
your spouse is not around
Do you call yourself a Christian when everybody is listening
Do you call yourself a Christian Jesus is Savior and Lord
Do you call yourself a Christian because you love your enemy
Do you call yourself a Christian because
He shed His blood for you
Call yourself Christian because you believe
He died, was buried, rose for you
Call yourself Christian because
He prepared a place in eternity for you
Call yourself Christian because you believed in
your heart and confessed with your mouth
What is a Christian

TYRA J. ROBINSON, SR.

AMEN

Amen to the brother raising them kids
Amen to the sisters giving new life the chance to live
We all walk the walk and talk the talk
But when it all ends no one wins
All the friends in the world can't change your life

You are keeping the faith
Blind faith if it be
But just if one Amen could be answered
Would God move the needle for little old me?

One more Amen let's see

FAITH—JUSTICE—MERCY

Faith a substance I hope for
Justice what hurt screams for
Mercy the thing one begs for
Mercy is gaining more than one can consume
Justice what a child looks for
Faith is believing that it is visible
Put them together you have to much of good for the blind
Too much of guilt for the seeing
They need mercy present to move on
They grasp for each other dependence of each other
I declare mercy, justice, faith, are vindicated

TYRA J. ROBINSON, SR.

THE WAIT IS OVER

I woke up that day, I had 7 hours left
I dreamt it
Waited for it
I found it
I reached to find my dream
Sometimes I didn't know what it meant

I spent 5 years plus with kids and no fuss
Looking for that someone to listen to and trust
So I waited a little longer to see what God was going to do
He really took His time I must say
Three plus years later He reshaped me His way

I didn't see it coming
But I could taste it real bad
Now the wait is over I'm glad

The wait is over
Load off my shoulder
Move the boulder
The wait is over

IT'S IN MY HANDS

It's in my hands the keys to my destiny
The way of money, fame, and fortune
It's in my hands the ability to succeed when all hope is lost
My hands would be empty as for heart distraught
My mind stuck in a rut

An yet it's in my hands
No I can't control my future
But if I'm going to get there it's me all the way
The haters and perpetrators and back stabbers are many
But them too are in my hands

My hands are big to some and to some very small
But just to have my hands full of power is not enough
Yes' that's what I'm saying and I ain't playing

It's all in my hands just because I'm in His hands

THANKSGIVING

T- Thinking of you

H- Hours we spend together

A- Adoration I give to you

N- Nothing is too hard for God

K- Knowledge we all share

S- Savior's birth

G- God's giving

I- Inspiration the word gives

V- Victory over the grave

I- Intimate with God

N- Navigation of the Holy Spirit

G- God is God all by Himself

TRUE PEACE AND JOY

My life has changed, has changed for the better
I now have true peace and joy
I understand why God allowed me to suffer
I now have true peace and joy
It was hard and painful to stay focus
I now have true peace and joy
Thank you Lord for your mercy and grace
I now have true peace and joy
I've come a long way and have a long way to go
I now have true peace and joy
My past is in the past, and my future is in front of me
I now have true peace and joy
Moving forward is where I've longed to be
I now have true peace and joy

ELIZABETH

TYRA J. ROBINSON, SR.

CAN IT HAPPEN FOR ME

Can it happen now or will it happen later
Can it happen for me
Can I become what I dreamed
Can I be what I believe

Will it happen for me
It should I'm honest
But the world is not kind
It should, I'm faithful

But the world would say other wise
Can it happen for me
Will it happen me
It will and can happen for me

MY MOUTH

When I open my mouth it speaks volumes
Whether making or resolving a problem
The pressure to stand leaves you alone
Sometimes I wish I spoke on the phone
I guess cause it's easier for me
Rather easier for the one I love to face me

I wish I was perfect and right
But last I checked I myself is a wreck
Yet my mouth is where the power of being a man comes out
Sometimes a person's tongue puts a man into position to be
cursed out

Yet I must not keep silent
For sake of family, in spite of many faults
I must continue to talk about what God has taught
I may not do it in the best of ways
But rest assured I mean it in a loving way

TYRA J. ROBINSON, SR.

So my mouth speaks volumes is I'm the only one listening
Please give me ears so my words won't become tears
I'm sorry if I hurt you
I'm just trying to love you best and sometimes I fail that test

Yet I won't give up until my dying day
For my mouth speaks volumes I must say
One day you say I should be silent
Yet that's when peace is lost and the kingdom suffers violence
Still I must open this little instrument to all I love

For its one of my smallest blessings from above

A Voice, A Soul, A Man Speaks

HOW TO KILL A GIANT

How to kill a giant
First you trust in the Lord
Call out his name and go stand in his face
But the giant going to think you crazy so keep your space

Look at him dead in the eyes
Reach for your faith
Let God fill the place
And give God the glory, cause this is the end of the story

God fights your battles
Put the enemy in your hand
Stand and profess you come in the name of the living God
Let the word of the Lord work on your behalf

Next the giant comes crashing down like a tree
Cut him at the knees, because you got the victory
So don't be surprised of the giants in your life
With God fighting your battles you never get rattled

So do be defiant
Self reliant
God will help and show you how to kill a giant!

HER SUBMISSION

Submit is a verb don't let her cut a nerve
It's a voluntary action that lets you serve
Submission is a choice we make give or take
It's what men want and women hate

Submission is what we must decide to do from the start
The decision to submit must first start inside the heart
Women or wives to be exact are afraid to submit
Because upon the profound to be kept in check

Their husbands use them only as can do's and what I say
The husband himself can't get it together to fully submitted to God
In reference to Christ, He doesn't neglect or ignore
Furthermore He gave his life, why not the husband for the wife

Her submission will come to him who is worthy
Are you hearing me this is not a mission my man
Homeboy my brother submit to God in win her heart
Her submission is one to cherish if you ask

Then her heart and love will be given to you and you'll will have
her submission

GODS MIRROR

When I get up in the morning to wash my face
I look in the mirror in see another face
This face isn't me as I thought to be

It talks to me and tells me about myself
One thing the mirror says to me a lot is listen
You're my child I love you and you belong to me

Sometimes the mirror is very friendly and encouraging
Sometimes the mirror makes me cry
Sometimes the mirror makes me feel ashamed and embarrassed

Why, because this beautiful mirror is all scratched up
Or is it me that's scared and the mirror hides my wombs
This shows my heart, soul, my mind, and everything that's inside

It wants to make me better—greater
Later now, yet I frown and close the mirror
Because every time I look in this mirror
I stand I stand naked yet fully clothed

I am not ashamed of what I do, say, or have become
This is the Spirit's mirror looking into my soul
God is looking at everyone
Everyone could use a look in God's mirror

TYRA J. ROBINSON, SR.

LIFE AND BAGGAGE

You accumulate it from the day of birth
The precious memories and the staples of their worth
All the learning experiences one will go through
Not just everybody even you

The struggles you'll go through
Will help shape you
The countless achievements that will heap upon you
Relationships will come and go

A friend who will be glue to you
In a friend who never knew you
You'll go from first to college
Stacks and loads of knowledge

As it is that life may have it
You might be a parent one day or two
But love must find marriage for you
Until then sometimes you'll feel its slackage

Just a small reminder that life is filled with baggage

Making the Ribbon

Million particles of thread
Pointed needles, holes in the head
The lighting of color
Thy connector of another
Go head pull one away
While someone pulls another
The beginning of something special is forming
It feels so warming
Whether you see the finish
Is entirely up to you
Not knowing what will come of…
Depends on both of you
You get to choose the color the line will make
You weave in, you weave out
Magical venture is coming about
You're taking this, you're taking that
They're taking that and taking this
It tightens the making of this special gift
Relative to a symbol one doesn't have the choice
Stay together long enough you get the proof

TYRA J. ROBINSON, SR.

Never forsaking all that you've given
Over the years you have evolved and shared
In the making of your RIBBON

A ribbon is to ends of linen. On each end is a man and a women and between them is miles of color. They are on the same team because the ribbon is perfectly woven, solid, and tied for a bow. Unity in a knot that's life and all it brings to people from opposite worlds and tying together their souls forever!

SUNDAY FEAST

It starts before I awake
It roars beneath my gut
I savor the taste that waters my mouth
If you don't know, I'll tell you what I'm talking about

It's butter biscuits
Greens and corn
Fried chicken and fish
All on my dish

Baked macaroni and cheese—smooth
The many different styles of rice oh please
Seafood salad, salmon that's baked
I haven't forgotten dessert so you must wait

Buttered down dinner rolls
So many meats to eat
The children enjoy it you can tell by the sound of their voices
Thanks Mom, good Mom, and even I good Honey delicious
Lord, I love after church Sunday

It unfolds with an early rise to give God the praise
Some entrees prepared before Sunday
Cake, cookies, peach cobbler and more
We have an excellent chef, Gracias

When it's all done
When it's time to eat
When we all meet
When we pray for the blessing over our meal to eat
I wait another week for the Sunday Feast

WE SHARE 9-11

Did those who died on 9-11 have a destiny or say
Did you see the attack from the planes hi-jacked
Crashed into the twin towers
Oh, the lives lost at a great cost
The children, parents, aunts, uncles, grandparents, and friends
We take a breath just to breathe even harder again
The state of shock that day
Sent the Nation straight to its knees
Pray, pray, pray, and pray they say
The passengers who risked their lives on the plane who
sacrificed for the many
They took the terrorist and the plane for a dive, Thank You
Thousands to be remembered on that day
How can you forget the reflection every year
Brings back the heartache, pain, and tears
Yet the strength was shown
We will not be afraid or intimidated
We're as confident as ever
Yet still with more challenges at home we face
Now as a Nation we face all kinds of threats but 9-11 we'll
never forget

Tyra J. Robinson, Sr.

We're still America, I say America
This beautiful country flaws and all
There none like America God Bless us all
For you past and present don't be surprised we honor you too
with Victory in our eyes
If you're still grieving it's ok, don't stop believing
The love that overflows from every life that matters, this is for
you too
We share and will remember you because you mattered in this life
We must go on, be it not alone
We'll have somebody to lean on
That hand we can't see in hopes of bringing you back
I'll hold on to Heaven, that's where my Savior is at
I must be real in times of unrest
Shortchanging myself won't mirror your best
So with 9-11 on the calendar every year we share in your memory
With humbleness and tears we wish you were still here
We must act in our world today
Lord God show us how to have a DEBT OF LOVE I PRAY

A PRAYER FOR MY WIFE

I've given her the ring
I've placed on her finger
Yet me saying I love you is not all she can bear
So what I'll do is offer up prayer

I'll pray for my wife
Because I love her
I'll pray on bended knee
My wife is my Queen

I'll pray for deliverance out of all life's distress
The way I pray, I'm at the throne boldly
I must focus, I'm thinking about what she told me
I'm here now, a moment of silence I crave

My hands are folded
My mind is stayed on the Lord
I pray I'm coming in truth
As I lift my wife up in prayer,
I'll cover her everywhere

I'll tell my GOD of her needs, wants, and desires
I ask HOLY SPIRIT set my heart on fire
I am very specific with things I can't tell you
My GOD answers prayers and that's the truth

In this life I'll never stop praying for my wife
I love her to the depth of my being
It's with GOD who's doing the leading
I pray for my wife because I love her

She is my Butterfly and a Sweetheart forever!

A Voice, A Soul, A Man Speaks

Why Do You Say No To Me

We gave our word to each other
We committed our lives on this journey
Why would I not lay down my life for you
Yet if I need you, you say no

You said no to me
And I felt ashamed
You said no to me as though you forgot my name
Am I yours and you are mines?
I say this must stop

Will you not answer my call
Will you say no to our favorite movie
Will you say no to sharing lights
There is just too many no's, it just isn't right

Why say no to me, I expect a yes
I need a yes like a river needs a waterfall to fill it
Yet my river is becoming a pond
Please one yes could balance the tide

Please I ask before you say no
Stop for a moment to rehearse your words
Because saying no to me would break me
Now I hesitate before I ask of a need

Why do you respond with no to me

TYRA J. ROBINSON, SR.

GRATITUDE

So, you're a gratitude and appreciation person
Gratitude never says it's all about me
Instead it says thank you and I care
Instead gratitude says I won't take anyone for granted

Like selfishness will
I say selfishness gets a reprimand everyday
Always worrying and thinking about herself
Selfishness has no power over brother gratitude

Gratitude says I love you to the giver
And won't take advantage of another
He stands firm and tall against his sister
Who claims to have changed over all

But gratitude won't become jealous or envious
They use to be close until selfishness came in
Yes she put an end to that

So gratitude let it show
Let someone know you're thankful and always deserving
So to gratitude don't go far
We always need to know where you are

WE SHARE 9-THESE MOMENTS

They are unique
They can happen in a twinkle of an eye
A timely smile
Walking the green mile

These special moments

The strong vibes
The silent love songs
The rainy memories
That stop time in the moment

These are the moments

All the sadness gone
The moments gone
The anger gone
Anxiety, fear, frustration, and doubt gone

All because someone says they care

These moments last forever
These moments happen when you least expect it
These moments expect them
These moments believe in them

Every moment has the possibility to be one of these
You just have to have to believe
And you will get

A MOMENT FOR YOU—LOVE

CPSIA information can be obtained
at www.ICGtesting.com
Printed in the USA
LVHW070738260723
753101LV00001B/3